DRUM TECHNIQUES OF

RUSH

Transcribed by Bill Wheeler

The drum arrangements in this folio were prepared under the supervision of Neil Peart.

Alfred Publishing Co., Inc.
16320 Roscoe Blvd., Suite 100
P.O. Box 10003
Van Nuys, CA 91410-0003
alfred.com

ISBN 10: 0-7692-5055-6
ISBN 13: 978-0-7692-5055-7

CONTENTS

MUSICAL DEFINITIONS
Terms used in this book

 This equation gives the definite tempo of the song and indicates that the speed of the note given in the equation is at that rate to a minute (i.e. 120 quarter notes are played in 1 minute).

Grace Notes - Undersized notes without computative value in the measure. The grace notes are to be played as close to the principle note as possible. The above applies to flams as well.

 Placed in the staff is an indefinite symbol of measures "rested." A number placed within or above the staff indicates the number of measures to be rested.

 Repeat the preceding measure in its entirety.

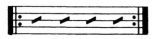 Repeat the measures within the repeat marks.

Repeat the preceding two measures in their entirety.

Play 1st ending, go back to repeat marks, then play through to 2nd ending. There can be an infinite number of endings.

 Fermata - placed under or over a note or rest, hold the note at pleasure.

> Accent - When a note is given special emphasis.

 Rolls are notated in this manner and are usually played as sixteenth note triplets or thirty-second notes, depending on the tempo. The note tied to the roll is to be played.

NOTES & RESTS

Notes:

Whole	Half	Quarter	Eighth	Sixteenth	Thirty-second
o	♩	♩	♪	♪	♪

Rests:

Whole	Half	Quarter	Eighth	Sixteenth	Thirty-second

Relative Value of Notes

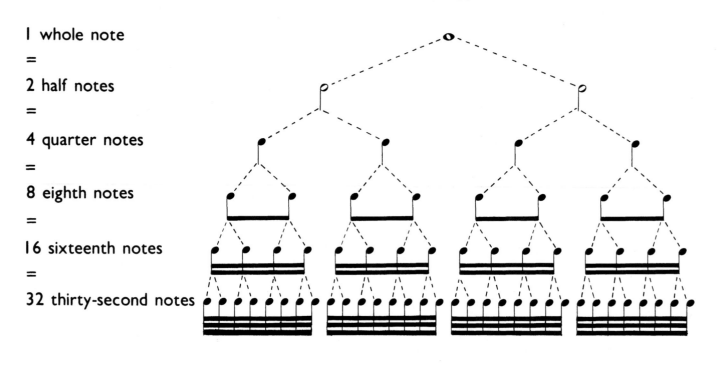

1 whole note
=
2 half notes
=
4 quarter notes
=
8 eighth notes
=
16 sixteenth notes
=
32 thirty-second notes

Dotted notes & Rests

Single dot
=

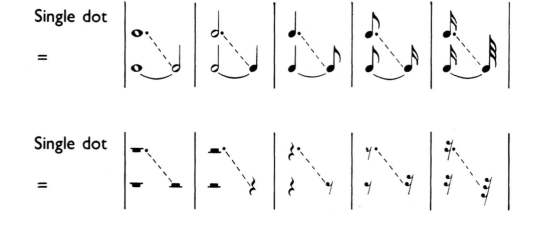

Single dot
=

ARTIFICIAL NOTES

Eighth Note Triplets

Two eighth notes are equal to one quarter note. Three eighth notes can also equal a quarter note as long as there is a "3" above or below the three eighth notes. This is an eighth note triplet.

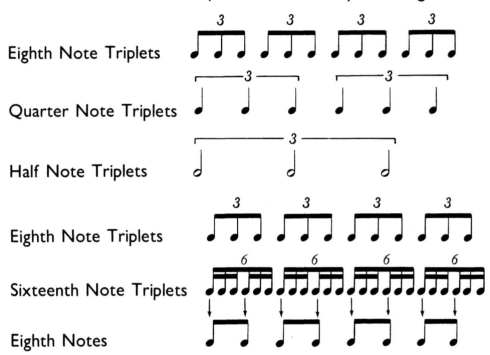

We will also see quarter note triplets and sixteenth note triplets. The examples below show the subdivision of triplets. Note the rhythmic alignment of the notes.

Eighth Note Triplets

Quarter Note Triplets

Half Note Triplets

Eighth Note Triplets

Sixteenth Note Triplets

Eighth Notes

WAYS OF COUNTING

There are many ways to count rhythms. Several are shown below:

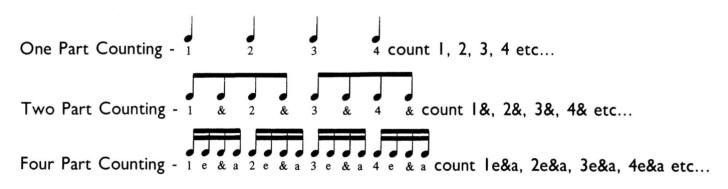

One Part Counting - 1, 2, 3, 4 count 1, 2, 3, 4 etc...

Two Part Counting - 1 & 2 & 3 & 4 & count 1&, 2&, 3&, 4& etc...

Four Part Counting - 1 e & a 2 e & a 3 e & a 4 e & a count 1e&a, 2e&a, 3e&a, 4e&a etc...

Triplet Counting -

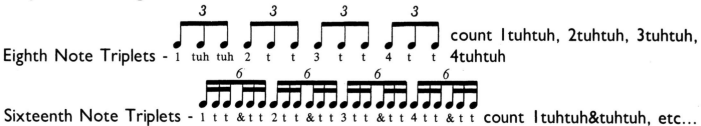

Eighth Note Triplets - 1 tuh tuh 2 t t 3 t t 4 t t count 1tuhtuh, 2tuhtuh, 3tuhtuh, 4tuhtuh

Sixteenth Note Triplets - 1 t t & t t 2 t t & t t 3 t t & t t 4 t t & t t count 1tuhtuh&tuhtuh, etc...

TIME SIGNATURES

The time (or tempo) in which the song is to be played is indicated by two numerals placed at the beginning. This is called the time signature. The upper numeral tells us the number of beats to be played in a measure. The lower numeral tells us the note (or rest) that receives the beat. For example:

4 = 4 beats to a measure.
4 = The quarter note receives one beat.

7 = 7 beats to a measure.
8 = The eighth note receives one beat.

7 = 7 beats to a measure.
16 = The sixteenth note receives one beat.

7 = 7 beats to a measure.
4 = The quarter note receives one beat.

DYNAMICS

Pianississimo - (ppp) very, very soft.

Pianissimo - (pp) very soft.

Piano - (p) soft.

MezzoPiano - (mp) moderately soft.

FortePiano - (fp) accent strongly, diminishing instantly to piano.

MezzoForte - (mf) moderately loud.

Forte - (f) loud.

Fortissimo - (ff) very loud.

Fortississimo - (fff) very, very loud.

Crescendo - gradually louder.

Decrescendo - gradually softer.

Ritard - gradually slower.

DRUM LEGEND

The fifth line on the staff represents any cymbal or percussion instrument and is designated by its symbol or full name.

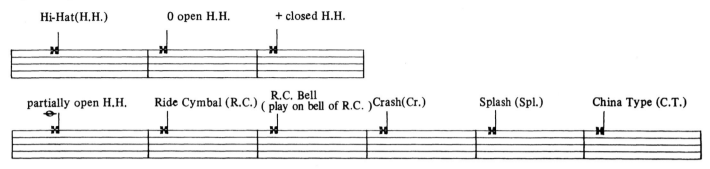

The first space above the staff, fifth line, fourth space and fourth line on the staff represent the 6", 8", 10" and 12" concert toms.

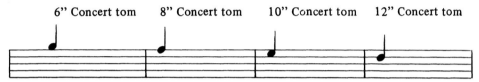

The third space on the staff represents the snare drum, timbales, cowbell and temple block.

*If more than one bell or block is being used they will be shown on the other lines or spaces according to the pitch of the instruments.

The third line, second space and second line represent the 12", 13" and 15" rack toms.

The first space on the staff represents the 18" floor tom.

The first line on the staff represents the bass drum(s)* and H.H. with foot.

*When the right and left bass drums are being used together they will be notated with a right (R) or a left (L).

Other Symbols:
Choke - quickly stop cymbal ringing by using your hand.
——————→ Continue playing unless otherwise notated.

THE TREES

Words by
NEIL PEART

Music by
GEDDY LEE and ALEX LIFESON

LA VILLA STRANGIATO

Words and Music by
GEDDY LEE, ALEX LIFESON
and NEIL PEART

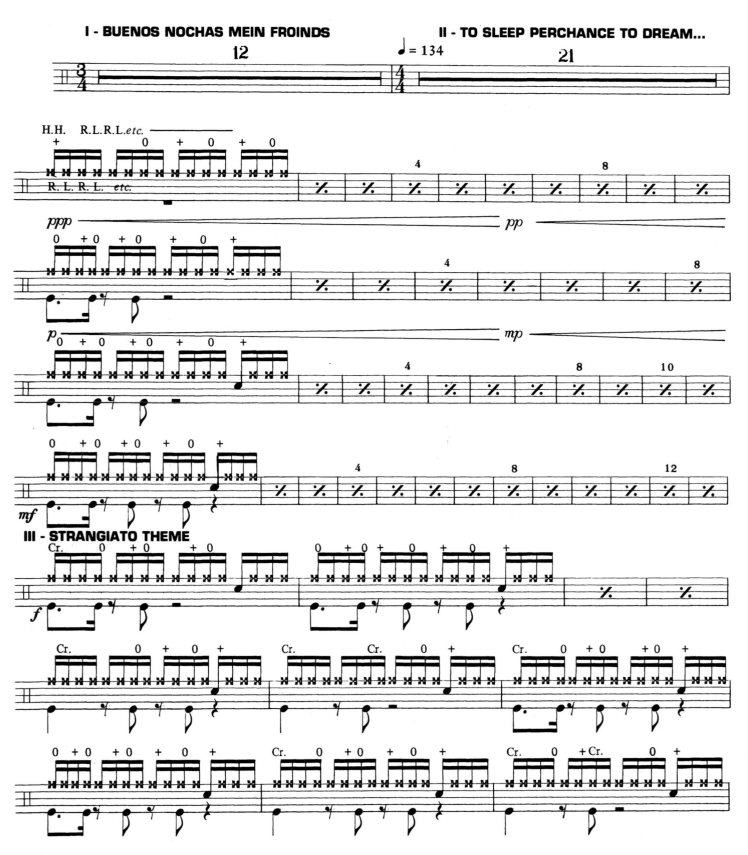

I - BUENOS NOCHAS MEIN FROINDS

II - TO SLEEP PERCHANCE TO DREAM...

III - STRANGIATO THEME

IV - A LERXST IN WONDERLAND

VI - THE GHOST OF THE ARAGON

VII - DANFORTH AND PAPE

VIII - THE WALTZ OF THE SHREVES

IX - NEVER TURN YOUR BACK ON A MONSTER!

X - MONSTERS! (REPRISE)

XI - STRANGIATO THEME (REPRISE)

XII - A FAREWELL TO THINGS

THE SPIRIT OF RADIO

Words by
NEIL PEART

Music by
GEDDY LEE and ALEX LIFESON

* ♩ = Timbales

FREE WILL

Words by
NEIL PEART

Music by
GEDDY LEE and ALEX LIFESON

* H.H. on 3rd & 4th repeat

ritard.

JACOB'S LADDER

Words by
NEIL PEART

Music by
GEDDY LEE and ALEX LIFESON

* The broken lines represent two measure phrases of 5/4 and 6/4 playing "on top" of the 4/4 synthesizer & vocal parts.

Improvise various percussion

mp

NATURAL SCIENCE

Words by
NEIL PEART

Music by
GEDDY LEE and ALEX LIFESON

TOM SAWYER

Words by
PYE DUBOIS and NEIL PEART

Music by
GEDDY LEE and ALEX LIFESON

RED BARCHETTA

Words by
NEIL PEART

Music by
GEDDY LEE and ALEX LIFESON

fade

YYZ

Music by
GEDDY LEE and ALEX LIFESON

*These four endings are taken from "Exit Stage Left".

LIMELIGHT

Words by
NEIL PEART

Music by
GEDDY LEE and ALEX LIFESON

*The broken lines in the above 6/8 part represent the drums playing a 4/4 rhythm "on top" of the 6/8 guitar pattern.

XANADU

Words and Music by
GEDDY LEE, ALEX LIFESON
and NEIL PEART

* This part is written in half time notation ($\tekspunt$ = 216)
**Make a gradual transition from double time ($\tekspunt$ = 268) to straight time ($\tekspunt$ = 134)

*Gradually slower

SUBDIVISIONS

Words by
NEIL PEART

Music by,
GEDDY LEE and ALEX LIFESON

NEW WORLD MAN

Words by
NEIL PEART

Music by
GEDDY LEE and ALEX LIFESON

DISTANT EARLY WARNING

Words by
NEIL PEART

Music by
GEDDY LEE and ALEX LIFESON

BETWEEN THE WHEELS

Words by
NEIL PEART

Music by
GEDDY LEE and ALEX LIFESON

* = Simmons